Dedication

This book is dedicated to the beloved *Imām* of our time (ʿaj). May Allah (swt) hasten his reappearance and help us to become his true companions.

Acknowledgments

Prophet Muḥammad (ṣ): The pen of a writer is mightier than the blood of a martyr.

True reward lies with Allah, but we would like to sincerely thank Sisters Iman Doroudi, Eman Abdul-Razzak, Nida Syed, Fatima Hussain, Sabika Mithani, Abeda Khimji, and Zainab Hussain. May Allah bless them in this world and the next.

Marḥūmīn Dedication

Please recite a *Sūrah al-Fātiḥah* for *Marḥūmah* Loraine Browdski Mirza, *Marḥūma* Seyda Zehra, *Marḥūma* Safiya Jaan Sultan, and the *marḥūmīn* of the Mazloum and Bhimji Families.

Disclaimer: Religious texts have not been translated verbatim so as to meet the developmental and comprehension needs of children.

Library of Congress Control Number: 2020925306

For permission requests, please write to the publisher at the address below.

Kisa Kids Publications
4415 Fortran Court
San Jose, CA 95134
(260) KISA-KID [547-2543]
info@kisakids.org

Hayaa's Chador

Written by Iman Doroudi

Illustrated by Eman Abdul-Razzak

Transliteration Chart

Arabic terms in this book have been transliterated according to the following guidelines*:

ء	a, i, or u (initial form)	ض	ḍ
ء	ʾ(medial or final form)	ط	ṭ
ا	a	ظ	ẓ
ب	b	ع	ʿ
ت	t	غ	gh
ث	th	ف	f
ج	j	ق	q
ح	ḥ	ك	k
خ	j	ل	l
د	d	م	m
ذ	dh	ن	n
ر	r	ه	h
ز	z	و	w
س	s	ي	y
ش	sh	ة	h (without iḍāfah)
ص	ṣ	ة	t (with iḍāfah)

ـَ	a	آ / ـَا / ىٰ	ā
ـِ	i	ـِي	ī
ـُ	u	ـُو	ū
		آ	ʾā (medial form)

*Please note that due to limitations, the transliteration is not 100% accurate in capturing tajwīd rules.

Preface

Prophet Muḥammad (ṣ):
Nurture and raise your children in the best way. Raise them with the love of the Prophets and the Ahl al-Bayt (ʿa).

Literature is an influential form of media that often shapes the thoughts and views of an entire generation. Therefore, in order to establish an Islamic foundation for the future generations, there is a dire need for compelling Islamic literature. Over the past several years, this need has become increasingly prevalent throughout Islamic centers and schools everywhere. Due to the growing dissonance between parents, children, society, and the teachings of Islam and the *Ahl al-Bayt* (ʿa), this need has become even more pressing. Al-Kisa Foundation, along with its subsidiary, Kisa Kids Publications, was conceived in an effort to help bridge this gap with the guidance of *ʿulamāʾ* and the help of educators. We would like to make this a communal effort and platform. Therefore, we sincerely welcome constructive feedback and help in any capacity.

The goal of *Hayaa's Chador* is to bring awareness to the *chador*, which is sometimes a foreign object to many, particularly those living in the West. The *chador* is not only deeply rooted in Islamic culture, but is also a profound way of being chaste and modest. The name of the protagonist in this story is Hayaa, which eloquently means the outward manifestation of modesty. The internal feeling of modesty is called *ʿiffah*, and this compels an individual to act, dress, and think with *ḥayāʾ* as they are aware of being in the presence of Allah. One external manifestation of this feeling is the chador, which is explored in this story. Hayaa sees the chador as a norm of society when she performs *ziyārah* and grows to love and adopt the *chador* herself.

We hope that you and your children enjoy these books and use them as a means to achieve this goal, *inshāʾAllāh*.

We pray to Allah to give us the strength and *tawfīq* to perform our duties and responsibilities.

With *Duʿās*,
Nabi R. Mir (Abidi)

Woosh!

Woosh!

Salāmun ʻalaykum! My name is Hayaa, and this is my *chador*! You put it on the top of your head, put your arms through the holes, and let it fall around you.

I got it when I visited the shrine of Imām Ḥusayn (‘a) in Karbala.

I wear it in Medina to visit my Prophet (ṣ) and his family.

I wear it for *ziyārah* in

Iraq,

Iran,

and Syria!

One day, I hope to wear a white chador for *Ḥajj*, but for now, I wear it to perform *‘umrah*!

It catches the air like a cape when I feel strong,

and it wraps around me when I need to
feel protected.

I wear my *chador* to the *masjid*,

to *majālis*,

and to Sunday School.

On the weekend, my Islamic Studies teacher, Sister Hamidah, talks about ḥijāb. She says that Allah (swt) asks us to wear ḥijāb, and because Allah created us, Allah knows what is best! She also says that covering up our bodies opens up our minds.

She says, “Wearing ḥijāb is like waving the flag of our faith, and wearing a chador is a more complete way to honor the important ladies of the Ahl al-Bayt (‘a)!”

SHOW AND
TELL
EXPO

On Monday, I take my *chador* to show and tell at school. I tell my friends all about it, and I show them how to wear it!
I say to the class, "Did you know my name means modesty? I think the *ḥijāb* and *chador* are just right for me!"

At home, *Baba* says, “Modesty is important for all people in the way we talk, dress, eat, behave, and more!”

My Mom adds, “The *chador* is an extra layer of *ḥijāb*. It is the best display of modesty on the outside.”

I love my *chador*. I love the way it covers me. It reminds me of my faith. I wear it for Allah.

I thank Allah for my beautiful blessings, my parents, my home, and even my *chador*! I thank Allah by promising to be a good Muslim.

Observing Ḥijāb

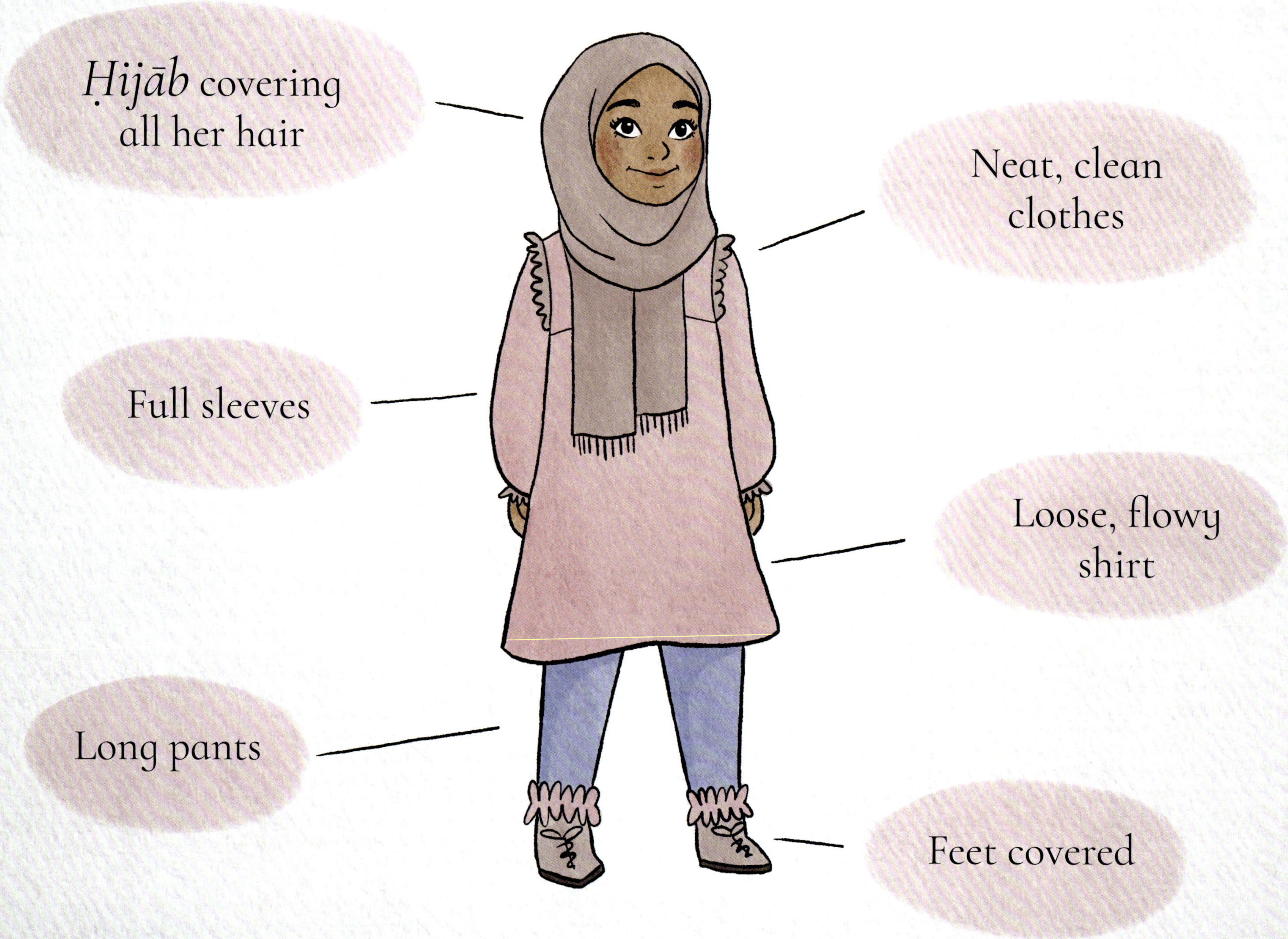

Glossary

(ṣ): Peace and blessings be upon Prophet Muḥammad (ṣ) and his family

(swt): All glory belongs to God, the Glorified and Exalted

(ʻa): Peace and blessings be upon him/her

(ʻaj): May God hasten his reappearance

Ahl al-Bayt: Divinely appointed family members of Prophet Muḥammad (ṣ)

Baba: Father

Chador: A large piece of cloth that is wrapped around the head and upper body, leaving only the face exposed, worn especially by Muslim women

Ḥajj: A pilgrimage to Mecca performed in the 12th Islamic month; it is obligatory on every Muslim once in his/her lifetime if certain conditions are met. Ḥajj is one of the most essential practices of Islam

Ḥijāb: A state of inner and outer modesty, often referring to the modest Islamic dress code

Imām: A divinely appointed leader, sometimes refers to a spiritual leader

Majālis: Gatherings

Masjid: Mosque

Salāmun ʻalaykum: Peace be upon you

Ziyārah: Visiting the house of Allah or the graves of the Noble Prophet (ṣ), the Imāms (ʻa), and other important personalities

ʻUmrah: An optional pilgrimage to Mecca that can be performed almost any time of the year